Animal

teNeues

teNeues

Portraits of 88 Animals & One Shy Enchanted Boy

Porträts
von 88 Tieren & einem scheuen verzauberten Jungen

—

Ritratti
di 88 animali & di un timido bambino incantato

introduction

————

Unlike a lot of people, it had never been my dream to write books. I never thought I could do it or that what I wrote would be interesting enough to be published. When teNeues, the publisher, asked me to put together books of my pet portraits, I started sketching and added my quirky scribble next to the images. And they decided to go global with the project. How could I ever have imagined that I would receive a message from a book retailer in New Zealand who had discovered my stories and told me they are on her list of top 3 favourite books.

While I was creating my artworks, the characters turned into real personalities and sometimes started to look like the people around me, some of them even appeared to be me. I was occasionally inspired by those I admired and other times I just wondered how people came to be so selfish or arrogant. I realised that I was jealous of those who annoyed me and it forced me to face my own shortcomings. Our acquaintance revealed secrets I was unaware of at the time.

I created ANIMAL during the toughest period of my recovery, trying to get back on my feet after a burnout. During the winter I stayed in the middle of the French countryside. It was cold and lonely but It gave me the time and space to think, sleep and try to take good care of myself. During this long winter my daily responsibility was a good walk though the fields with Fidele, a beautiful brown-eyed golden labrador, who loyally waited at my door every day around 4.00 pm.

When Spring arrived, everything changed completely. Covid 19 had altered the world. Everyone experienced the fear and an instinct for survival that I had already been living with for months. Living an isolated existence didn't seem so bad after all when the world was on fire. Observing from a safe distance was very interesting and gave me more inspiration to create remainder of my animal characters.

TEIN LUCASSON

Anders als viele andere Menschen hatte ich nie davon geträumt, Bücher zu schreiben. Ich hätte nie gedacht, dass ich das könnte oder dass das, was ich schrieb, interessant genug sein könnte, um veröffentlicht zu werden.

Als der Verlag teNeues auf mich zukam und vorschlug, meine Tierportraits zu Büchern zusammenzustellen, fing ich an, Skizzen zu machen und schrieb daneben meine skurrilen Gedanken dazu auf – und sie beschlossen, das Projekt länderübergreifend anzugehen. Wie hätte ich mir je vorstellen können, einmal eine Nachricht von einer Buchhändlerin in Neuseeland zu erhalten, die auf meine Geschichten gestoßen war und mir erzählte, ich gehöre zu ihren drei beliebtesten Autoren?

Während ich meine Bilder erstellte, verwandelten sich die Tiere in echte Persönlichkeiten und sahen manchmal fast so aus wie die Leute um mich herum. Manche davon schienen sogar ich selbst zu sein. Hin und wieder fühlte ich mich inspiriert durch die, die ich mochte, und dann wieder fragte ich mich, wie jemand so selbstsüchtig oder arrogant sein konnte. Mir wurde bewusst, dass ich auf diejenigen neidisch war, die mich nervten, und das zwang mich dazu, mich meinen eigenen Unzulänglichkeiten zu stellen. Unsere Bekanntschaften legen Geheimnisse offen, deren man sich oft nicht gleich bewusst ist.

Animal entstand während der schwierigsten Phase meiner Erholung nach einem Burnout, als ich versuchte, wieder auf die Beine zu kommen. Die Wintermonate verbrachte ich in Frankreich mitten auf dem Lande. Es war kalt und einsam, aber das gab mir die Zeit und den Raum, nachzudenken, zu schlafen und zu versuchen, mich gut um mich zu kümmern. Während dieses langen Winters bestand meine tägliche Aufgabe darin, einen ausgedehnten Spaziergang über die Felder zu machen mit Fidele, einem wunderschönen Labrador mit goldbraunen Augen, der Tag für Tag verlässlich gegen 16 Uhr an der Tür schon auf mich wartete.

TEIN LUCASSON

introduzione

U A differenza di molte persone, scrivere libri non è mai stato un mio sogno. Non ho mai pensato che avrei potuto farlo, o che quello che avrei scritto sarebbe stato abbastanza interessante da essere pubblicato.

Quando teNeues, l'editore, mi chiese di raccogliere i miei ritratti di animali in alcuni libri, iniziai a metterli insieme aggiungendo bizzarri commenti di mio pugno accanto alle immagini — e la casa editrice decise di lanciare il mio progetto a livello globale. Non avrei mai potuto immaginare di ricevere un messaggio da una rivenditrice di libri neozelandese che aveva scoperto le mie storie e mi informava che si trovavano nella top 3 della sua lista di libri preferiti.

Durante la realizzazione dei miei disegni, le figure cominciarono a trasformarsi in personaggi veri e propri e ogni tanto ad assomigliare a persone attorno a me; in alcuni casi mi sembrava persino di vedere me stesso. A volte venivo ispirato da persone che ammiravo, altre mi chiedevo semplicemente come la gente finiva per diventare così egoista ed arrogante. Mi resi conto di essere invidioso delle persone che mi infastidivano e questo mi spinse ad affrontare le mie carenze. La conoscenza di queste persone ha portato a galla segreti di cui all'epoca ero all'oscuro.

Realizzai ANIMAL durante il periodo più difficile della mia guarigione, mentre cercavo di rimettermi in piedi dopo un esaurimento. Era inverno e vivevo nel mezzo della campagna francese. Faceva freddo e mi trovavo in un posto remoto, ma questo mi diede tempo e spazio per pensare, dormire e provare a prendermi cura di me stesso. Durante questo lungo inverno, il mio compito quotidiano era quello di fare una bella passeggiata attraverso i campi assieme a Fidele, uno splendido Labrador color miele dagli occhi marroni che ogni giorno intorno alle 16 aspettava fedelmente davanti alla mia porta.

Con l'arrivo della primavera, tutto cambiò completamente. Il Covid-19 aveva alterato il mondo. Tutti quanti provarono la paura e quell'istinto di sopravvivenza con cui io stavo già convivendo da mesi. Vivere isolato non mi sembrava poi così male in un momento in cui il mondo era in fiamme. Osservare da una distanza di sicurezza è stato molto interessante e mi ha fornito ulteriore ispirazione per il resto dei miei personaggi animali.

TEIN LUCASSON

№ 1
Juliana

———

With big crocodile tears in her eyes, she
reported him as a missing person. She had
taken what she needed, and now it was time
for him to leave the stage. Like always,
Juliana was focussing on her bigger plan.

———

Mit dicken Krokodilstränen in den Augen
meldete sie ihn als vermisst. Sie hatte
genommen, was sie brauchte, und nun war es
Zeit für ihn, die Bühne zu verlassen. Wie immer
fokussierte sich Juliana auf ihren größeren Plan.

———

Con grosse lacrime di coccodrillo negli occhi,
denunciò la sua scomparsa. Si era presa quello
che le serviva, e ora era giunto il momento che
lui uscisse di scena. Come sempre, Juliana si
stava concentrando sul suo grande progetto.

———

nº 2
Hella

———

They think she is hysterical and overreacting.
Ella has stopped defending herself from
them. She is sensitive and likes to stay that
way. Wise Ella distances herself and likes to
keep her joys small.

———

Alle glauben, sie sei hysterisch und würde
übertrieben reagieren. Ella hat es aufgegeben,
sich vor ihnen zu rechtfertigen. Sie ist sensibel
und möchte auch so bleiben. Die kluge Ella
bleibt auf Distanz und gibt sich mit kleinen
Freuden zufrieden.

———

Di lei pensano che sia isterica ed esagerata.
Ella ha smesso di difendersi da queste persone.
È sensibile e le piace rimanere tale. La saggia
Ella prende le distanze e ama le piccole gioie.

———

№ 3
Armina

———

She is the keeper of secrets, she carries many,
some of them darker than her kind heart can
handle. At midnight she trusts them to the moon.
She needs to get some sleep. She knows they are
safe with the moon and understands that some
of them must be kept in the dark.

———

Sie ist die Geheimnishüterin, und es sind viele
Geheimnisse, die sie bewahrt, manche davon
düsterer als ihr freundliches Herz ertragen kann.
Um Mitternacht vertraut sie sich dem Mond an.
Sie muss etwas Schlaf finden. Sie weiß, beim
Mond sind ihre Geheimnisse gut aufgehoben.
Und sie weiß, dass manche besser im Dunklen
bleiben müssen.

———

È la custode di segreti, ne porta molti, alcuni
più oscuri di quanto il suo cuor gentile possa
sopportare. A mezzanotte li affida alla luna — lei
ha bisogno di dormire un po'. Sa che con la luna
i segreti sono al sicuro e comprende che alcuni
devono essere tenuti al buio.

———

№ 4
Lars

———

Dad and his only aunt had another stupid fight,
so it was better not to be in touch for a while.
He was happy when dad's friend offered to be his
"fake-uncle." This way he learned to be creative
if adults are acting childishly.

———

Schon wieder hatten sein Vater und seine einzige
Tante einen albernen Streit, also war es besser,
ihnen eine Weile aus dem Weg zu gehen. Er freute
sich, als der Freund seines Vaters sich ihm als
„Ersatzonkel" anbot. So lernte er, kreativ zu sein,
wenn sich die Erwachsenen kindisch benahmen.

———

Il papà e la sua unica zia stavano avendo un altro
stupido litigio, quindi era meglio starsene alla
larga per un po'. Fu contento quando l'amico del
babbo si offrì di fargli da "finto zio". In questo
modo imparò a essere creativo quando gli adulti
assumevano comportamenti infantili.

———

nº 5
Polly

———

There is no more room for her in the place
she once called "home." Others with secret
agendas made the decisions. She'd tried to stay
and hoped they heard her scream for help.
Will she be creative enough to find another
place she calls home?

———

Es gibt keinen Platz mehr für sie an jenem Ort,
den sie einst „Zuhause" nannte. Andere mit
geheimen Plänen trafen die Entscheidungen.
Sie versuchte zu bleiben und hoffte, jemand
würde ihren Ruf nach Hilfe hören. Würde sie
genug Kreativität aufbringen können, um
einen anderen Ort zu finden, den sie
Zuhause nennen kann?

———

Non c'è più spazio per lei nel posto che un tempo
chiamava "casa". Altre persone con piani segreti
avevano deciso tutto. Aveva cercato di restare
sperando che la sentissero gridare aiuto. Sarà
abbastanza creativa da trovare un altro posto
da chiamare casa?

———

№ 6
Nel

———

You have just entered her territory. Her tongue is sharp and her view limited. She is harmless if you leave her be. She has never been able to see the world from another perspective.

———

Du hast soeben ihr Territorium betreten. Ihre Zunge ist scharf, ihre Perspektive eingeengt. Lässt man sie in Ruhe, stört sie niemanden. Sie war nie in der Lage, die Welt aus einem anderen Blickwinkel zu betrachten.

———

Siete appena entrati nel suo territorio. La sua lingua è tagliente e la sua vista limitata. È innocua se lasciata in pace. Non è mai stata capace di vedere il mondo da un'altra prospettiva.

———

nº 7
sean

———

He had always been a silent observer of others.
They must never have realized how much
they had taught him about whom he absolutely
didn't want to become.

———

Er war immer schon ein stiller Beobachter
der anderen gewesen. Sie sind sich wohl nie
bewusst geworden, wie viel sie ihm darüber
beigebracht hatten, wie er auf gar keinen
Fall werden wollte.

———

Era sempre stato un silenzioso osservatore
degli altri. Non devono essersi mai resi conto
di quanto gli fossero stati maestri nel fargli
capire chi non voleva assolutamente
diventare.

———

№ 8
Aras

———

He knew this day would come. Time to give
up his role as the boss. He always planned to
leave in silence so as not to be laughed at.
He didn't want them to see a respected leader
become old and senile.

———

Er wusste, dieser Tag würde kommen.
Es war Zeit, sich von seiner Führungsrolle zu
verabschieden. Er hatte schon lange geplant,
ohne viel Aufhebens abzutreten, damit
niemand über ihn lachen würde. Sie sollten
nicht erleben, wie ein angesehener Leader
alt und senil wurde.

———

Sapeva che questo giorno sarebbe arrivato.
Era ora di rinunciare al suo ruolo di capo.
Aveva sempre pensato di andarsene in silenzio,
in modo da non essere deriso. Non voleva
che vedessero un capo stimato diventare
vecchio e senile.

———

№ 9
chet

———

He was a handsome rogue and he knew it.
But he got hooked on the hunt. Stupid Chet lost
the love of is life because of his uncontrollable
hormones. Mrs. Cheet was searching for
someone real.

———

Er war ein attraktiver Strolch und das wusste er.
Aber er konnte das Jagen nicht lassen. Wegen
seiner unkontrollierbaren Hormone verlor der
dumme Chet die Liebe seines Lebens. Mrs. Cheet
war auf der Suche nach jemand Echtem.

———

Era un mascalzone di bell'aspetto e lo sapeva.
Ma prese il vizio della caccia. Lo stupido Chet
ha perso l'amore della sua vita a causa dei suoi
incontrollabili ormoni. Quello che la signora
Cheet cercava era una persona vera.

———

№ 10
Benji

———

He was born as an afterthought. He always
wondered why they burdened themselves with
another mouth to feed. On a beautiful morning
after a very deep sleep he found a scar on his
belly and suddenly everything made sense.

———

Er wurde als Nachzügler geboren. Er hatte
sich immer gefragt, warum sie es sich angetan
hatten, noch einen Esser mehr sattkriegen zu
müssen. Eines schönen Morgens wachte er nach
einem sehr tiefen Schlaf auf mit einer Narbe
über seinem Bauch, und auf einmal ergab
alles einen Sinn.

———

Nacque come un ripensamento. Si chiedeva
sempre perché si fossero dati la pena di un'altra
bocca da sfamare. Una splendida mattina, dopo
un sonno profondissimo, scoprì una cicatrice sul
suo ventre e all'improvviso tutto ebbe un senso.

———

№ 11
Jackie

———

Grandma helped Little Jackie to develop green fingers. In her village, on Saturdays, she brought her free-spirited elderly friends her homegrown herbal remedies. Jackie had to be inventive to save up for later.

———

Die Großmutter sorgte dafür, dass Little Jackie einen grünen Daumen entwickelte. In ihrem Dorf versorgte sie samstags ihre freigeistigen älteren Freunde mit ihren selbstgemachten pflanzlichen Heilmitteln. Jackie musste erfinderisch sein, um später zurechtzukommen.

———

La nonna aveva aiutato il piccolo Pelo Jackie a maturare il pollice verde. Nel suo villaggio, il sabato, portava ai suoi vecchi amici dallo spirito libero rimedi a base di erbe coltivate da lei. Pelo Jackie dovette essere inventivo per risparmiare per il futuro.

———

№ 12

cilo

———

He was born into a family of hunters.
While playing, he became friends with the deer
living in the forest. Whenever his family planned
a hunt, he sent his dog with a sweet warning
message the night before.

———

Er wurde in eine Familie von Jägern
hineingeboren. Beim Spielen freundete er sich
mit den Tieren im Wald an. Immer, wenn die
Familie eine Jagd plante, schickte er am Abend
zuvor seinen Hund hinaus mit einer leisen
Warnung.

———

Era nato in una famiglia di cacciatori.
Durante i suoi giochi, divenne amico dei cervi
che vivevano nella foresta. Ogni volta che la sua
famiglia organizzava una battuta di caccia,
la notte prima mandava il suo cane a portare
un dolce messaggio di avvertimento.

———

№ 13
Julien

———

He really hoped that after a nose job they would
all realize that the stage was where he belonged.
He soon found out that this was not enough
to make his dream come true. One beautiful
morning, just like any other day, he will look in
the mirror for hours and ask himself, "Vanity,
what have you done to me?"

———

Er hatte sehr gehofft, nach einer Nasenkorrektur
würden alle erkennen, dass die Bühne sein Platz
war. Er fand schon bald heraus, dass dies nicht
ausreichte, um seinen Traum wahrwerden zu
lassen. Eines schönen Morgens, an einem Tag
wie jeder andere, wird er sich stundenlang im
Spiegel betrachten und sich fragen: „Eitelkeit,
was hast du mir angetan?"

———

Sperava davvero che dopo una plastica al naso
tutti si sarebbero resi conto che il palcoscenico
era il suo posto. Ben presto scoprì che questo
non bastava per realizzare il suo sogno. Una
bella mattina, di un giorno come tanti altri, si
guarderà allo specchio per ore chiedendosi:
"Vanità, che cosa mi hai fatto?".

———

№ 14
vito

———

After recovering from a trauma, he hoped happy
thoughts would return. Unfortunately an empty
and numb feeling came over him instead.
He realized that forward was his new direction.
New memories have to be made so happiness
can return.

———

Nach der Überwindung eines Traumas
hatte er die Hoffnung, es würden sich
wieder glückliche Gedanken einstellen.
Unglücklicherweise überkam ihn jedoch
stattdessen ein leeres und dumpfes Gefühl. Ihm
wurde klar, dass „Vorwärts" seine neue Richtung
war. Neue Erinnerungen müssen entstehen,
damit das Glück zurückkehren kann.

———

Dopo essersi ripreso da un trauma, sperava
che tornassero i pensieri felici. Purtroppo,
invece, gli venne una sensazione di vuoto e di
intorpidimento. Si rese conto che andare avanti
era la sua nuova direzione. Occorre creare nuovi
ricordi perché la felicità possa tornare.

———

№ 15
viv

———

Instead of sobbing over her burnt down
home and looking at what she has lost,
she is resilient and builds an even better
house than before.

———

Anstatt über ihr abgebranntes Haus zu
jammern und nur das zu sehen, was sie
verloren hat, lässt sie sich nicht unterkriegen
und baut ein noch besseres Haus als zuvor.

———

Invece di piangere sulla sua casa divorata
dalle fiamme e guardare a ciò che ha perso,
lei è forte e costruisce una casa ancora più
bella di prima.

———

№ 16
sherida

————

She knows how to create a little magic to
turn special kids into grown-ups who think
like she does. Her bigger plan is to turn the
world into a more beautiful place.

————

Sie hat ein magisches Händchen dafür,
aus bestimmten Kindern Erwachsene werden
zu lassen, die so denken wie sie. Ihr großes Ziel
ist es, die Welt zu einem besseren
Ort zu machen.

————

Sa come compiere una piccola magia
per trasformare i bambini speciali in
adulti che la pensano come lei. Il suo grande
progetto è quello di trasformare il mondo
in un posto migliore.

————

n⁰ 17
Giovanni

———

He is very selective but,when you are in with
him, his friendship is unconditional. He is
someone to count on. He enjoys the simple
things. Life is great if you just let everything be.

———

Er ist sehr wählerisch, aber kommt man an ihn
heran, ist seine Freundschaft bedingungslos. Er
ist jemand, auf den man bauen kann. Er genießt
die einfachen Dinge. Das Leben ist großartig,
wenn man die Dinge einfach laufen lässt.

———

È molto selettivo, ma se diventi dei suoi, la sua
amicizia è incondizionata. È una persona su cui
poter contare. Gli piacciono le cose semplici.
La vita è magnifica se solo si lascia che le cose
vadano per il loro verso.

———

№ 18
Pieter-chistiaan

———

His rich parents always spoiled him and never
took the time to teach him manners or morals.
As long as he was loyal to his college mates, he
saw himself as decent. All those below him in
society needed to learn their place.

———

Seine reichen Eltern hatten ihn immer
verwöhnt und sich nie Zeit dafür genommen,
ihm Umgangsformen und Moralvorstellungen
beizubringen. Er selbst betrachtete sich als
anständig, solange er seinen Studienkollegen
gegenüber loyal war. Alle, die gesellschaftlich
unter ihm standen, mussten lernen, wo ihr
Platz war.

———

I suoi ricchi genitori lo avevano sempre
viziato e non si erano mai presi il tempo di
insegnargli le buone maniere e i principi morali.
Gli bastava dimostrarsi leale nei confronti
dei suoi compagni di università per sentirsi
una persona rispettabile. Tutti quelli che
si trovavano sotto di lui nella scala sociale
dovevano imparare a restare al loro posto.

———

nº 19
Hervé

———

He knows about change and is able to speak wisely about it to those who are about to change. He likes to show them a different point of view. Some things in life are difficult to digest. Helping others makes him feel good.

———

Er kennt sich aus mit Veränderungen und kann gut mit jenen darüber sprechen, die vor Wandlungen im Leben stehen. Er zeigt ihnen gern einen anderen Blickwinkel auf. Manche Dinge sind schwer zu verdauen. Wenn er anderen hilft, fühlt er sich gut.

———

Sa che cosa vuol dire cambiare ed è in grado di parlarne con saggezza alle persone che si accingono a farlo. Gli piace mostrare loro un punto di vista diverso. Alcune cose nella vita sono difficili da digerire. Aiutare gli altri lo fa sentire bene.

———

№ 20
Edith

———

Her life before seemed like a movie that
passed in fast forward. She doesn't know
what to expect from here on. Can she escape or
push a button to become invisible?

———

Ihr vorheriges Leben erschien ihr wie ein
Film im Schnellvorlauf. Sie weiß nicht, was
nun auf sie zukommen wird. Kann sie allem
entfliehen oder einen Knopf drücken, um
unsichtbar zu werden?

———

La sua vita precedente le sembrava un film
fatto scorrere veloce. Non sa cosa aspettarsi
da qui in poi. Può fuggire o premere un
pulsante per diventare invisibile?

———

№ 21
Jennifer

———

She wished she had listened to her heart a long
time ago, when it told her to become a yoga
teacher. At the time, she chose security and
continued working around the clock. Now that
she has been fired, it hurts to discover that her
former colleagues are teaching yoga.

———

Sie wünschte, sie hätte schon vor langer Zeit
auf ihr Herz gehört, als es ihr empfahl,
Yogalehrerin zu werden. Damals entschied sie
sich für die Sicherheit und arbeitete weiter
rund um die Uhr. Jetzt, nachdem ihr gekündigt
wurde, tut es weh zu sehen, dass ihre früheren
Kollegen Yoga unterrichten.

———

Le piacerebbe aver ascoltato il suo cuore
tanto tempo fa, quando le diceva di diventare
un'insegnante di yoga. All'epoca, optò per
la sicurezza continuando a lavorare senza
interruzione. Ora che è stata licenziata,
le fa male scoprire che i suoi ex colleghi
insegnano yoga.

———

№ 22
Dietrich

———

He knows one day he could be as big as
the leaders he looks up to. He practices being
rude and ruthless and tells others what to do.
He was made to do this job!

———

Er weiß, dass er eines Tages auch so groß sein
kann wie die Führungspersönlichkeiten,
zu denen er hinaufschaut. Er übt sich darin,
grob und rücksichtslos zu sein, und sagt
anderen, was zu tun ist. Dieser Job ist
seine Bestimmung!

———

Sa che un giorno potrebbe essere grande
come i capi che ammira. Si esercita a essere
crudele e spietato e dice agli altri cosa fare.
È fatto per questo lavoro!

———

№ 23
Fran

———

She was happy when her husband left her.
He had never really been nice to her. He is
someone else's problem now, and she is glad
to be able to move on.

———

Sie war erleichtert, als ihr Mann sie verließ.
Er war nie wirklich nett zu ihr gewesen. Jetzt
ist er das Problem einer anderen und sie ist
froh, nach vorne blicken zu können.

———

Fu contenta quando il marito la lasciò.
Non era mai stato veramente gentile nei suoi
confronti. Ora lui è il problema di qualcun
altro e lei è felice di poter voltare pagina.

———

nº 24+25
Adeline & Florence

———

They had been friends since high school. After their kids flew the nest, they were left with their lazy disrespectful husbands. They didn't have to think long to decide to live together and open a tea room. Happiness is a choice and only given to the brave and fearless.

———

Sie waren Freundinnen seit ihrer Zeit in der Oberschule. Nachdem ihre Kinder dem Nest entflohen waren, blieben sie zurück mit ihren faulen, rücksichtslosen Ehegatten. Sie kamen ohne viel Nachdenken zu dem Entschluss, zusammenzuziehen und einen Teesalon zu eröffnen. Glück ist eine Entscheidung und wird nur jenen gewährt, die sich als tapfer und furchtlos erweisen.

———

Erano amiche dai tempi del liceo. Dopo che i loro figli avevano lasciato il nido, restarono con i loro mariti pigri e irrispettosi. Non dovettero pensarci a lungo per decidere di vivere assieme e aprire una sala da tè. La felicità è una scelta ed è concessa solo ai coraggiosi e impavidi.

———

№ 26
Henry

———

"No" has always been his favorite word.
It even created his job as a life coach for him.
He teaches "givers" the amazing power "no"
has to disappoint "takers."

———

„Nein" war immer schon sein Lieblingswort.
Er baute darauf sogar seine Arbeit als Life Coach
auf. Er bringt „Gebern" bei, welch erstaunliche
Kraft das Wort „Nein" hat, um „Nehmer" zu
enttäuschen.

———

"No" è sempre stata la sua parola prediletta,
a lei deve persino il suo mestiere di maestro
di vita. Lui insegna a "chi dà" l'incredibile potere
che il "no" ha di deludere "chi prende".

———

———

Great looks were given to others. He knew
he needed to attract attention in a completely
different way. He started to act like he knew it
all and added long words to his vocabulary.
Before he realized it, others started to respect
him. He got what he had always wanted
and lived happily ever after, knowing nothing
of what really mattered.

———

Mit gutem Aussehen waren andere gesegnet.
Er wusste, er musste auf ganz andere Weise die
Aufmerksamkeit an sich ziehen. Er begann, so
zu tun, als wüsste er alles und ergänzte seinen
Wortschatz um lange Wörter. Noch bevor er
selbst sich dessen bewusst war, wurde er immer
mehr respektiert. Er bekam, was er immer
gewollt hatte und lebte glücklich bis an das Ende
seiner Tage – ohne die geringste Ahnung zu
haben, was wirklich zählte.

———

Il bell'aspetto era stato dato in dono ad altri.
Sapeva che lui doveva attirare l'attenzione in
un modo completamente diverso. Cominciò
a comportarsi da saccente e arricchì con dei
paroloni il suo vocabolario. Prima che se ne
rendesse conto, gli altri iniziarono a rispettarlo.
Ottenne ciò che aveva sempre voluto e visse
per sempre felice e contento, non sapendo
nulla di ciò che contava davvero.

———

nº 28
Lamar

———

He is good at reading people. With his weird
sense of humor and enormous sensitivity, he
can bring very bad news and make it feel like
sunshine. He can't take away the problem, but
helps others to start dealing with it.

———

Er ist geschickt darin, Leute zu durchschauen.
Mit seinem eigenwilligen Sinn für Humor und
seinem großen Einfühlungsvermögen gelingt es
ihm, schlechte Neuigkeiten mitzuteilen und das
Ganze wie Sonnenschein wirken zu lassen.
Er kann zwar Probleme nicht wegzaubern,
aber anderen dabei helfen, nach und nach
besser damit umzugehen.

———

È bravo a capire le persone. Con il suo strano
senso dell'umorismo e la sua enorme sensibilità,
sa portare notizie pessime e farle sentire
come un raggio di sole. Non può cancellare il
problema, ma aiuta gli altri a iniziare
ad affrontarlo.

———

She knew how it worked, at one moment she
was a noble and caring mum, but when the
glucose levels in her blood dropped, she was
ready to murder a whole village.

Sie wusste, wie es ablief. In dem einen Moment
war sie eine großmütige und fürsorgliche
Mutter, aber wehe, ihr Blutzuckerspiegel ging in
den Keller, dann könnte sie ein ganzes
Dorf ermorden.

Sapeva come funzionava: un attimo prima era
una mamma nobile e premurosa, ma quando i
livelli di glucosio nel suo sangue precipitavano,
era pronta a uccidere un intero villaggio.

*JOSEP*H

———

The sea was his mistress and loved him as
wildly as he loved her. Friends warned him that
untamed love can become seriously dangerous,
and so it did. His remains were found a few days
after with a sweet smile on his face.

———

Das Meer war sein Meister, beide verband eine
gegenseitige wilde Liebe. Die Freunde hatten ihn
gewarnt, dass unbändige Liebe sehr gefährlich
werden kann, und so kam es dann auch. Man
fand seine sterblichen Überreste einige Tage
später – mit einem sanften Lächeln im Gesicht.

———

Il mare era la sua amante ed entrambi si
amavano selvaggiamente. Gli amici lo avevano
avvertito che l'amore indomito può essere
molto pericoloso, e così fu. Il suo corpo fu
rinvenuto qualche giorno dopo, sul suo viso
un dolce sorriso.

———

№ 31
Lorenzo

———

He was selected to follow the rules and
make others obey. When the rules changed
unexpectedly, he, like the others, got very
confused. From that moment, he has chosen
his own rules in what is good or wrong.

———

Es war seine Aufgabe, die Regeln zu befolgen
und dafür zu sorgen, dass andere gehorsam
waren. Als sich unerwarteterweise die Regeln
änderten, war er, genau wie die anderen,
sehr verwirrt. Von da an folgte er seinen
eigenen Regeln, um gut zu sein.

———

Fu scelto per seguire le regole e farle rispettare.
Quando le regole cambiarono inaspettatamente,
lui, come gli altri, ne fu molto confuso.
Da quel momento ha scelto le proprie regole
nel fare del bene.

———

———

He counted the hearts he broke and counted
the money he stole. Hurting others just felt good.
He wasn't able to care about their feelings.
Kenneth knew what real pain was, because he
felt it the moment his father left him with his
lunatic mother.

———

Er zählte die Herzen, die er gebrochen hatte,
und er zählte das Geld, das er gestohlen hatte.
Andere zu verletzen fühlte sich einfach gut
an. Er war nicht fähig, sich um ihre Gefühle
Gedanken zu machen. Kenneth wusste, was
echter Schmerz war, er hat ihn erlebt, als
sein Vater ihn mit seiner verrückten Mutter
zurückgelassen hatte.

———

Contava i cuori che spezzava e i soldi che
rubava. Ferire gli altri gli dava una bella
sensazione. Non era capace di preoccuparsi
dei loro sentimenti. Kenneth seppe cosa
fosse il vero dolore, poiché lo sentì nel
momento in cui suo padre lo lasciò con la
madre malata di mente.

———

nº 33
vinny

———

He had always doubted the intentions of
sunflowers. No one could be so cheerful and
happy all the time. They must be overreacting or
just superficial. One summer he watched them
from germination to flowering, and he learned
there is nothing wrong with pure and simple
happiness.

———

Er hatte immer an den Absichten der
Sonnenblumen gezweifelt. Nichts und niemand
konnte jemals ununterbrochen so fröhlich
und glücklich sein. Entweder mussten sie
übertreiben oder aber oberflächlich sein. Eines
Sommers beobachtete er sie von der Keimung
bis zur Blüte und erlebte dabei, dass nichts
falsch ist an purem und reinem Glück.

———

Ha sempre dubitato del vero intento dei girasoli.
Nessuno poteva essere sempre così allegro
e felice. Dovevano avere reazioni esagerate
o essere semplicemente superficiali. Un'estate
li osservò dalla germinazione alla fioritura,
e imparò che non c'è niente di sbagliato nella
pura e semplice felicità.

———

———

He knew he had everything: looks, intelligence
and a great personality. No wonder reproducing
himself was the most important thing on his
to-do list. Too bad he didn't invest the time to
become an inspiring parent, someone to really
look up to.

———

Er wusste, er hatte alles: gutes Aussehen,
Intelligenz und eine große Persönlichkeit.
Kein Wunder also, dass Fortpflanzung auf seiner
To-do-Liste ganz oben stand. Zu schade nur,
dass er nicht die Zeit investierte, ein
inspirierender Vater zu sein, jemand, zu
dem man hochschauen konnte.

———

Sapeva di avere tutto: un bell'aspetto, intelligenza
e una grande personalità. Nulla da stupirsi
se riprodursi fosse in cima alla sua lista delle
cose da fare. Peccato che non dedicò del tempo
a diventare un bravo genitore, qualcuno da
prendere veramente a modello.

———

№ 35
Mimoun

———

He was easily distracted. The rest of the group didn't understand what made his brain jump from one subject to another. For him, it all made logical sense. Connecting the dots was something he had done all of his life.

———

Er ließ sich leicht ablenken. Die anderen der Gruppe verstanden nicht, wieso sein Kopf immer von einem Thema zum anderen sprang. Für ihn dagegen ergab alles einen Sinn. Die Punkte zu verknüpfen war etwas, das er sein Leben lang getan hatte.

———

Si distraeva facilmente. Il resto del gruppo non capiva cosa facesse saltare la sua mente da un argomento all'altro. Per lui, tutto aveva un senso logico. Collegare i punti era una cosa che aveva fatto per tutta la vita.

———

nº 36
Priscilla

———

She doesn't feel like she belongs. Her parents like to show off their perfection. They want her to dress up nicely. Priscilla wishes she could teach them the difference between looking good and being good.

———

Sie hat nicht das Gefühl dazuzugehören. Ihre Eltern stellen gern zur Schau, wie vollkommen sie sind. Sie möchten, dass sie sich schön anzieht. Priscilla wünscht sich, ihnen den Unterschied klarmachen zu können zwischen gut aussehen und gut sein.

———

Non si sente a suo agio. Ai suoi genitori piace mettere in mostra la propria perfezione. Vogliono che lei si vesta bene. Priscilla vorrebbe poter insegnare loro la differenza tra l'essere belli fuori e l'essere belli dentro.

———

№ 37
zlatko

———

Some call him lazy. He knows how hard he
used to work and learned that working so hard
could never be all there is to life. He no longer
cares what others think; those with opinions are
on the top of his list to avoid.

———

Manch einer nennt ihn faul. Er weiß genau,
wie hart er früher gearbeitet hat, und er
hat begriffen, dass es nicht alles im Leben
sein konnte, so hart zu arbeiten. Es ist ihm
mittlerweile egal, was andere denken —
diejenigen mit vorgefassten Meinungen stehen
ganz oben auf der Liste derer, die es zu
meiden gilt.

———

Alcuni lo definiscono pigro. Si ricorda di quanto
duramente era solito lavorare in passato e
ha imparato che la vita non può essere solo
lavorare così duro. Non gli importa più di quello
che pensano gli altri; quelli pronti a dire il
proprio parere sono in cima alla sua lista
delle persone da evitare.

———

nº 38
Elias

———

Power was all that interested him. Not a spark
of humor was to be found in his system. Results,
discipline and order were all that mattered.
There were no tears when he passed away.

———

Macht war alles, was ihn interessierte. Nicht
ein Funken Humor war bei ihm zu entdecken.
Ergebnisse, Disziplin und Ordnung waren alles,
was zählte. Als er starb, flossen keine Tränen.

———

Il potere era l'unica cosa che lo interessava.
Non c'era una briciola di umorismo nel suo
universo. Di conseguenza, disciplina e ordine
erano tutto ciò che contava. Nessuno versò
lacrime quando scomparve.

———

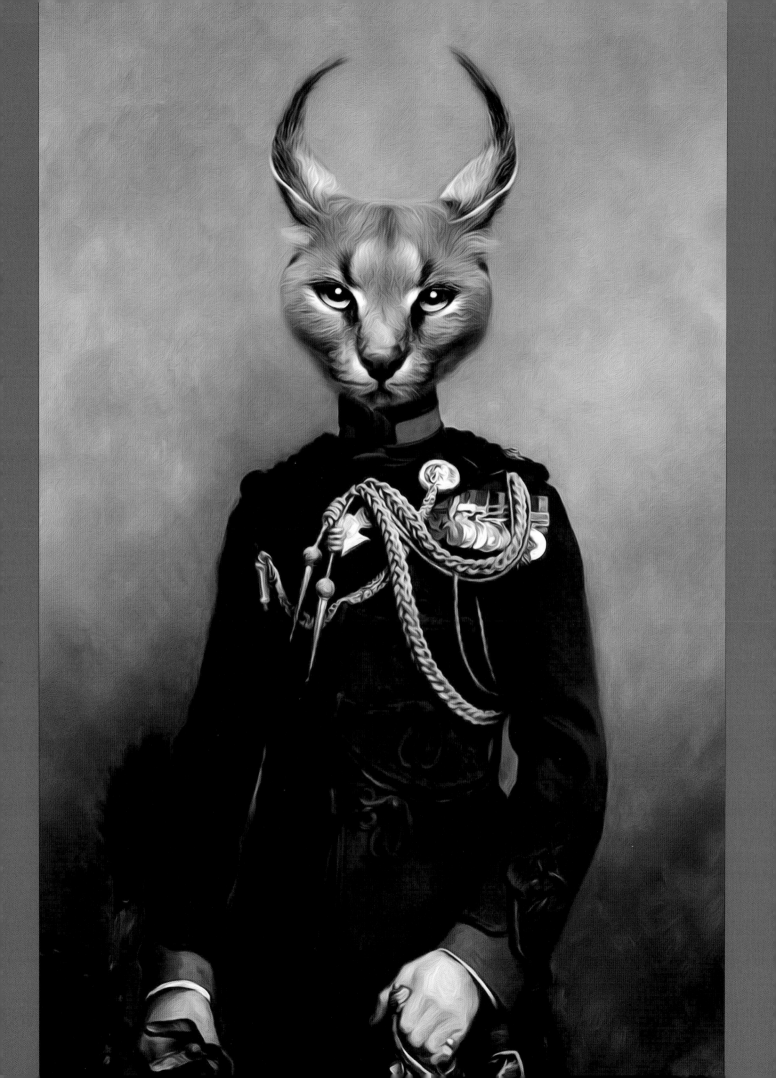

———

Since she escaped from her violent husband,
she has found solace in the spiritual world and
proudly founded a self-help group for victims.
Her new direction is all about burning incense
sticks, creating dreamcatchers and wild
dances around a fire.

———

Seit sie ihrem gewalttätigen Ehemann
entkommen ist, findet sie Trost in der
spirituellen Welt und hat stolz eine
Selbsthilfegruppe für Opfer gegründet.
Jetzt dreht sich alles um Räucherstäbchen,
das Basteln von Traumfängern und wilde
Tänze rund um ein Feuer.

———

Da quando è scappata dal marito violento,
ha trovato conforto nel mondo spirituale e ha
fondato con orgoglio un gruppo di auto-aiuto
per le vittime. Ora ciò che conta nella sua vita
è accendere bastoncini d'incenso, realizzare
acchiappasogni e ballare disinibita intorno
a un fuoco.

———

№ 40
Emanuel

———

He was a journalist, and felt the urge to report
the truth. He knew that his audience only liked
to hear stories they could relate to based on
half-truths. So he abandons his profession and
starts to write children's stories about a land that
doesn't exist.

———

Er war Journalist und es drängte ihn danach,
die Wahrheit zu berichten. Er wusste aber,
dass sein Publikum nur zu gern Dinge hörte,
die sie mit auf Halbwahrheiten beruhenden
Geschichten in Verbindung bringen konnten.
Daher gab er seinen Beruf auf und begann,
Erzählungen für Kinder zu schreiben, über
ein Land, das es nicht gibt.

———

Era giornalista, e sentiva il bisogno di raccontare
la verità. Sapeva che al suo pubblico piaceva
ascoltare solo storie basate su mezze verità.
Così decide di abbandonare la sua professione
e inizia a scrivere storie per bambini su una
terra che non esiste.

———

nº 41
youssef

He had always read books about great
philosophers. He admired their vision and
wanted to think like them. But when he became
wise himself, he noticed reality wasn't as pretty
as he had thought it was.

Er hatte immer schon Bücher über große
Philosophen gelesen. Er bewunderte ihren
Weitblick und wollte denken wie sie. Mit
zunehmender eigener Weisheit jedoch stellte
er fest, dass die Wirklichkeit gar nicht so schön
war, wie er immer gedacht hatte.

Aveva sempre letto libri su grandi filosofi.
Ammirava la loro visione del mondo e
desiderava pensare come loro. Ma quando
divenne saggio lui stesso, si accorse che la realtà
non era così bella come pensava fosse.

№ 42
Ritsu

The happiest he had ever been was on his way
to nowhere. He was curious about meeting
new people. New beginnings sounded so much
better than solving the difficult mess he had
left behind. He realized that he was going in the
right direction when looking back was no longer
important to him.

Nie war er so glücklich wie auf seinem Weg ins
Nirgendwo. Er brannte auf neue Begegnungen.
Neuanfänge klangen so viel verheißungsvoller
als das schwierige Durcheinander aufzulösen,
dass er hinter sich gelassen hatte. Dass es die
richtige Richtung war, wurde ihm klar, als der
Blick zurück ihm nichts mehr bedeutete.

Felice come non mai, procedeva senza meta.
Era curioso di conoscere nuove persone. I nuovi
inizi sembravano molto più facili di risolvere
il complicato pasticcio che si era lasciato alle
spalle. Si rese conto che stava andando nella
direzione giusta quando guardare al passato
per lui non era più importante.

№ 43
Jay

———

He was not the brightest diamond in the class, but he already knew what he wanted to become when he grew up: influencer or vlogger just like his idols. "And if that doesn't work?" the teacher asked. "I'll marry someone rich," he replied. The teacher smiled, nodded and moved on.

———

Er war nicht der hellste Stern der Klasse, aber er wusste schon damals, was er später werden wollte. Influencer oder Vlogger, genau wie seine Idole. „Und wenn das nicht klappt?", fragte der Lehrer. „Dann heirate ich jemanden mit Geld", antwortete er. Der Lehrer lächelte, nickte und ging weiter.

———

Non era il più brillante della classe, ma sapeva già cosa avrebbe voluto diventare da grande: influencer o vlogger, come i suoi idoli. "E se non funziona?", chiese l'insegnante. "Sposerò una persona ricca", rispose lui. L'insegnante sorrise, annuì e andò avanti.

———

№ 44
veronique

————

She was a trophy wife, but her late husband
didn't invest in her emotionally. After his
passing, he left her with a great fortune,
but she was lacking the spark to create a
great life of her own.

————

Sie war eine Trophäenfrau, aber ihr
verstorbener Mann hatte sich emotional nicht
wirklich auf sie eingelassen. Er hinterließ ihr
nach seinem Tod ein großes Vermögen, ihr fehlte
jedoch der richtige Gedanke, um sich ein eigenes
erfüllendes Leben aufzubauen.

————

Era una moglie "trofeo", ma il suo defunto marito
non investì su di lei a livello emotivo. Dopo la
sua morte, le lasciò una grande fortuna, ma a
lei mancava la scintilla per dare inizio a una
splendida vita tutta sua.

————

№ 45
Irving

———

Despite being a natural born leader, he still had
to fight his way to the top. He was smart enough
to maintain his position by spotting young
talent and eliminating them before they became
serious competition.

———

Obwohl er eine geborene
Führungspersönlichkeit war, musste er immer
noch um seinen Weg nach ganz oben kämpfen.
Er war smart genug, seine Position zu sichern,
indem er junge Talente aufspürte, die er dann
loswurde, bevor sie eine ernsthafte Konkurrenz
darstellten.

———

Pur essendo un leader nato, dovette comunque
lottare per arrivare in cima. Fu abbastanza
scaltro da mantenere la sua posizione,
individuando i giovani talenti ed eliminandoli
prima che diventassero seri competitori.

———

————

Friends never stayed, and groups excluded him.
His choice of good or bad faded when playing
too many video games. Right or wrong became
a matter of heads or tails. Right never seemed to
have embraced him, and wrong seemed
way more fun.

————

Freunde blieben nie lange und Gruppen
schlossen ihn aus. Seine Wahrnehmung von
Gut und Böse verblasste, wenn er zu viele
Videospiele spielte. Richtig oder falsch wurde
eine Frage von Kopf oder Zahl. Das Richtige
schien nie an ihn herangekommen zu sein und
das Falsche schien sehr viel mehr Spaß
zu bringen.

————

Gli amici non restavano mai, e i gruppi lo
escludevano. Il suo discernere tra bene e
male veniva meno quando giocava troppo ai
videogiochi. Giusto o sbagliato diventava una
questione di testa o croce. Sembrava non aver
mai abbracciato il giusto, e le cose sbagliate
parevano molto più divertenti.

————

———

It was a long and lonely ride to get him
to where he wanted to be. Because of his
insecurities, he became a self-declared
specialist. Everyone who doubted or dared to
critcize him had to find another purpose in life.
He and only he deserved to work for the king.

———

Es war ein langer und einsamer Weg gewesen,
dorthin zu gelangen, wo er hin wollte.
Aufgrund seiner Unsicherheit entwickelte er
sich zu einem selbsternannten Spezialisten.
Jeder, der an ihm zweifelte oder es wagte,
ihn zu kritisieren, musste sich eine andere
Aufgabe im Leben suchen. Er und nur er
verdiente es, für den König zu arbeiten.

———

Fu un viaggio lungo e solitario per arrivare
dove voleva. A causa delle sue insicurezze,
divenne uno specialista autodichiarato.
Chiunque dubitasse di lui o osasse criticarlo,
doveva trovare un altro scopo nella sua vita.
Lui e solo lui meritava di lavorare per il re.

———

n⁰ 48
Thomas

———

He loved looking at the stars at night and
wondered if they were friends or foes. Did one
with a brighter spark or closer to the moon have
a higher status? He imagined stars must
be wiser and above all of this.

———

Er liebte es, nachts die Sterne zu betrachten,
und fragte sich, ob sie wohl Freunde oder
Feinde waren. Hatte einer, der heller leuchtete
oder näher am Mond war, einen höheren
Stellenwert? Er stellte sich vor, dass die
Sterne klüger und all diesen Fragen überlegen
sein mussten.

———

La notte amava guardare le stelle e chiedersi
se fossero amiche o nemiche. Quelle più lucenti
o più vicine alla luna erano più prestigiose?
Si immaginava le stelle dotate di maggior
saggezza e superiori a tutto questo.

———

№ 49
Charlotte

———

They call her arrogant, but she is anything but that. They probably had expectations she didn't know about. She is happy, has sweet friends and is not interested in romance with another jealous lover.

———

Sie sagen, sie sei überheblich, aber das Gegenteil ist der Fall. Wahrscheinlich hatten sie Vorstellungen, von denen sie nichts wusste. Sie ist glücklich, hat nette Freunde und keinerlei Interesse an einer Romanze mit einem weiteren eifersüchtigen Liebhaber.

———

La definiscono arrogante, ma è tutto tranne questo. Probabilmente avevano aspettative di cui lei non era a conoscenza. Lei è felice, ha amici cari e non è interessata a una storia d'amore con un altro amante geloso.

———

nº 50
samir

———

Being there unconditionally for whomever
needed help is, for him, like breathing air. Giving
a hand to those who needed it was a pleasure.
But when he needed help himself he realized
how exceptional his attitude had been.

———

Da zu sein, bedingungslos, wenn jemand ihn
brauchte, egal wer, war für ihn wie die Luft
zum Atmen. Jenen zur Hand zu gehen, die Hilfe
brauchten, war ihm eine Freude. Als er dann
aber selbst Hilfe brauchte, wurde ihm klar, wie
außergewöhnlich seine Haltung war.

———

Esserci incondizionatamente per chiunque
necessitasse di aiuto era per lui come respirare
l'aria. Dare una mano a chi aveva bisogno era un
piacere. Ma quando fu lui ad aver bisogno
di aiuto, si rese conto di quanto eccezionale
fosse stato il suo atteggiamento.

———

nº 51
sophie

———

Innocent Sophie knows how to impress.
She gets away with dubious matters. After
a few failures she has learned to think before
acting. Life can be fun but can never be
considered a game.

———

Die unschuldige Sophie war sehr geschickt
darin, andere zu beeindrucken. Auch bei
fragwürdigen Dingen kommt sie gut davon.
Nach ein paar Misserfolgen hat sie gelernt
nachzudenken, bevor sie handelt. Das Leben
kann ein Spaß sein, sollte aber niemals als
ein Spiel betrachtet werden.

———

L'innocente Sophie sa come fare buona
impressione. Nelle situazioni dubbie la fa franca.
Dopo qualche sbaglio ha imparato a pensare
prima di agire. La vita può essere divertente,
ma non può mai essere considerata un gioco.

———

№ 52
Leroy

He knows what he did, but he didn't realize at
the time how much pain it would cause. He had
said, "Sorry." To him, waiting for the returned
favor seemed just a matter of time. The fear of
not knowing when was an invention by karma.

Er weiß, was er getan hat, war sich aber
damals nicht bewusst, wie viel Schmerz
das verursachen würde. Er hatte gesagt:
„Es tut mir leid." Die Reaktion schien nur eine
Frage der Zeit zu sein. Die Sorge, nicht zu
wissen, wann sie kommen würde, war eine
Erfindung des Karmas.

Sa quello che ha fatto, ma allora non si
rendeva conto di quanto dolore avrebbe causato.
Aveva detto "Mi dispiace". A lui, aspettare che
il favore venisse contraccambiato sembrava
solo una questione di tempo. La paura di non
sapere quando è stata un'invenzione del karma.

nº 53
Glenn

———

At a very young age, he discovered he was
gifted. By taking big risks, never giving up and
being completely dedicated, winning was all
that mattered. He developed the right mentality
to become a very talented businessman.

———

Schon in jungem Alter stellte er fest, eine
Begabung zu haben. Er riskierte viel, gab
niemals klein bei und engagierte sich voll und
ganz. Zu gewinnen war dabei für ihn immer das
Einzige, was zählte. So entwickelte er die richtige
Mentalität für einen talentierten Geschäftsmann.

———

In giovanissima età, scoprì di essere dotato.
Correndo grandi rischi, non arrendendosi mai
e dedicandosi anima e corpo, vincere era l'unica
cosa che contava. Sviluppò la mentalità giusta
per diventare un uomo d'affari di grande talento.

———

———

He loved looking at himself in the mirror.
He was thrilled when he found an app on his
phone to show the world how amazing his life is.
But deep inside he hopes someone will cure
him of this desperate need for attention.

———

Er liebte es, sich im Spiegel zu betrachten.
Er war begeistert, wenn er mit einer App auf
seinem Smartphone der Welt zeigen konnte, was
für ein tolles Leben er führte. Ganz tief in seinem
Inneren jedoch hofft er, dass irgendjemand
ihn von diesem verzweifelten Bedürfnis nach
Aufmerksamkeit befreien wird.

———

Amava guardarsi allo specchio. Era entusiasta
quando sul suo telefonino ha trovato una app
per mostrare al mondo quanto magnifica fosse
la sua vita. Ma nel profondo spera che qualcuno
lo guarisca dal suo disperato
bisogno di attenzione.

———

nº 55
carol

―――

"Do you remember when we really loved each
other?" asked her husband. She didn't answer.
"Me neither," he said. "We wasted each other's
time, but I liked showing you off to my mates."
Some time later he died and left a letter saying
he had donated everything to charity.
She realized with hindsight that she should
have made better choices.

―――

„Kannst du dich daran erinnern, als wir
beide uns wirklich liebten?", fragte ihr Mann.
Sie antwortete nicht. „Ich mich auch nicht",
sagte er. „Wir haben gegenseitig unsere Zeit
verschwendet, aber ich habe mich immer gern
mit dir bei meinen Freunden gezeigt." Einige
Zeit später starb er und hinterließ einen Brief,
in dem er angab, alles für einen wohltätigen
Zweck spenden zu wollen. In später Einsicht
wurde ihr klar, dass sie klüger hätte
wählen sollen.

―――

"Ti ricordi quando ci amavamo davvero?",
chiese il marito. Lei non rispose. "Nemmeno io",
disse lui. "Abbiamo solo perso il nostro tempo,
ma mi piaceva vantarmi di te davanti ai miei
amici". Qualche tempo dopo lui morì, lasciando
una lettera in cui diceva di aver donato tutto in
beneficienza. Con il senno di poi, lei si rese conto
che avrebbe dovuto fare scelte migliori.

―――

№ 56
jon

———

From a young age he had very big dreams,
but after failing a few times he gave up and
got depressed. He didn't realize these failures
were just tests to find out how much he
wanted them to come true.

———

Als Kind hatte er immer sehr große Träume
gehabt, nach einigen Fehlschlägen jedoch gab
er auf und wurde depressiv. Es war ihm nicht
klar gewesen, dass diese Fehlschläge lediglich
Tests waren um herauszufinden, wie viel es ihm
bedeutete, dass seine Träume wahr würden.

———

Fin da giovane, nutriva grandi sogni, ma dopo
aver fallito alcune volte, ci rinunciò e cadde
in depressione. Non si rese conto che quegli
insuccessi erano solo prove per scoprire quanto
desiderava che i suoi sogni si realizzassero.

———

nº 57
Mavra

Every morning the cock did his best to wake her up as early as possible. She was not a morning person, and one day she decided to have him prepared for dinner. By the next morning, she had fallen into an eternal sleep.

Morgen für Morgen tat der Hahn sein Bestes, Mayra so früh wie möglich aufzuwecken. Sie war kein Morgenmensch und so beschloss sie eines Tages, ihn sich zum Mittagessen zubereiten zu lassen. Am nächsten Morgen war sie in einen ewigen Schlaf gefallen.

Ogni mattina il gallo faceva del suo meglio per svegliarla il più presto possibile. Lei non era una persona mattiniera, e un giorno decise di farlo preparare per cena. Il mattino seguente, era caduta in un sonno eterno.

nº 58
Donny

———

They always make jokes about him and tell him
that he will never be like them. It took years
before he realized that being like them would be
too easy. They triggered bigger dreams in him.

———

Sie machen sich immer über ihn lustig und
sagen ihm, dass er nie so sein wird wie sie. Es
dauerte Jahre, bevor ihm klar wurde, dass es viel
zu einfach wäre, so wie sie zu sein. Sie hatten
ihn zu größeren Träumen angestachelt.

———

Lo prendono sempre in giro e gli dicono che non
sarà mai come loro. Ci sono voluti anni perché
si rendesse conto che essere come loro sarebbe
stato troppo facile. Sono loro ad aver suscitato in
lui sogni più grandi.

———

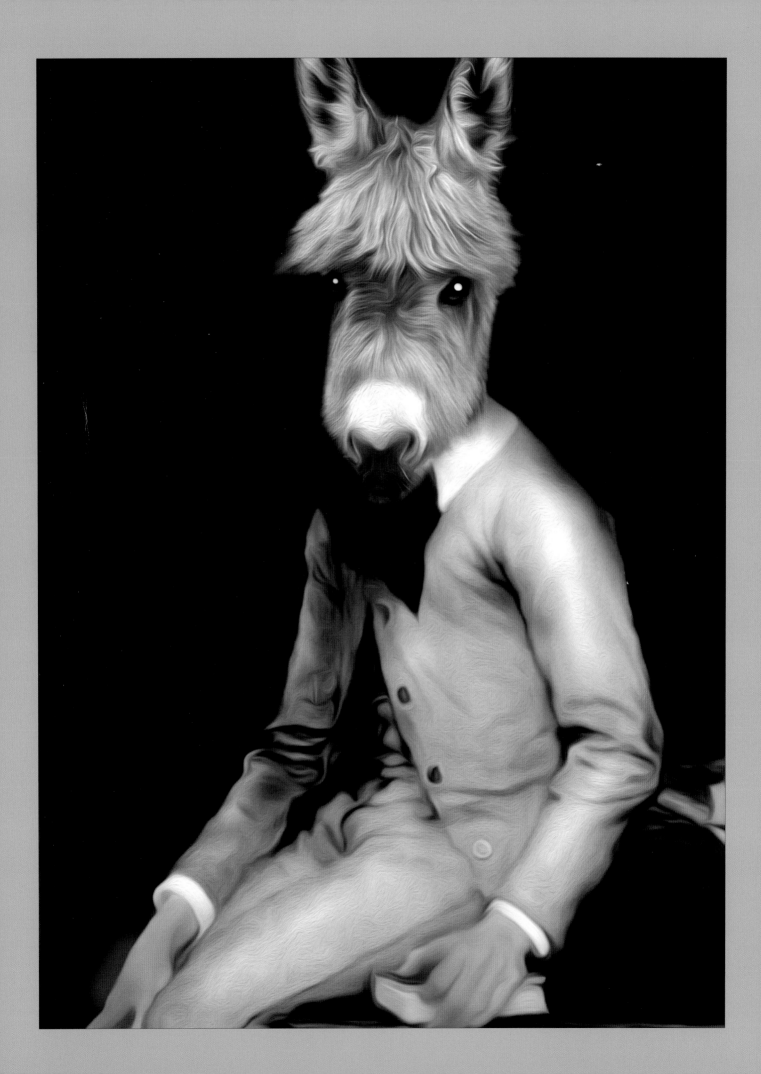

№ 59
Mona

———

She looked into his eyes and was happy they
had stayed together through thick and thin, and
not just because it was a habit. Leaving each
other without fixing what went wrong would
have been too easy. She wouldn't have been
complete without him.

———

Sie schaute in seine Augen und war froh,
dass sie zusammen durch dick und dünn
gegangen waren – und dies nicht nur aus einer
Gewohnheit heraus. Sich zu verlassen, ohne das
geradezurücken, was schief gelaufen war, wäre
zu einfach gewesen. Ohne ihn war sie nicht
vollständig.

———

Lei lo guardò negli occhi ed era felice che fossero
rimasti assieme nel bene e nel male, e non solo
per abitudine. Lasciarsi senza sistemare quello
che era andato storto sarebbe stato troppo facile.
Non sarebbe stata completa senza di lui.

———

nº 60
caro

———

She is a good friend, someone who is always there for others. She has never had a lover or a relationship. Her talent is that she can listen as if she really cares. If only they knew she uses their pain to write those heartbreaking poems.

———

Sie ist eine gute Freundin, eine, die immer für andere da ist. Sie hatte nie einen Liebhaber oder eine Beziehung. Ihr Talent liegt darin, so zuhören zu können, als wäre es ihr wirklich wichtig. Wenn die anderen nur wüssten, dass sie sich ihr Leid zunutze macht, um jene herzzerreißenden Gedichte zu schreiben.

———

È una buona amica, una persona sempre a disposizione degli altri. Non ha mai avuto un amante o una relazione. Il suo talento è quello di saper ascoltare come se le importasse davvero. Se solo sapessero che usa il loro dolore per scrivere quelle poesie strazianti.

———

№ 61
Rico

———

He never expected to find love. Good looks
were given to others who thought it was enough
to find a nice girl. But he has yet to realize that
the best girls are interested in someone with
a heart of gold.

———

Er war nie davon ausgegangen, Liebe zu finden.
Mit gutem Aussehen waren andere gesegnet,
die dachten, es reiche aus, ein nettes Mädchen
zu finden. Was ihm noch klar werden muss,
ist, dass die besten Mädchen an jemandem mit
einem Herz aus Gold interessiert sind.

———

Non si aspettava di trovare l'amore. Un aspetto
attraente era stato dato in dono ad altri, che
pensavano fosse sufficiente per trovare una
bella ragazza. Ma non ha ancora capito che le
ragazze migliori hanno interesse per chi ha un
cuore d'oro.

———

№ 62
Norman

―――

When the sun was around he was the happiest
version of himself. The sun was his healer.
It changed ugly things into beauty, especially
at sunrise or sunset. He only discovered the
nasty side when he looked into the mirror and
saw the wrinkly man staring back at him.

―――

Wenn die Sonne schien, war er die glücklichste
Version seiner selbst. Die Sonne war seine
Heilerin. Sie verwandelte hässliche Dinge in
Schönheit, ganz besonders bei Sonnenauf- oder
Sonnenuntergang. Die schlechte Seite entdeckte
er erst, als er in den Spiegel schaute und den
faltigen Mann sah, der ihn anblickte.

―――

Quando c'era il sole, emergeva il lato più
ridente di lui. Il sole era il suo balsamo: cambiava
le cose brutte in belle, specialmente all'alba e al
tramonto. Si rese conto del lato oscuro quando,
guardandosi allo specchio, vide un uomo
rugoso che lo fissava.

―――

№ 63
Jonathan

———

He saw himself as a regular guy with very
average desires. He liked spending time with
his beloved and a good coffee in the morning.
He didn't realize that many must have envied
his normality.

———

Er betrachtete sich selbst als ganz normalen
Typ mit sehr durchschnittlichen Bedürfnissen.
Er mochte es, Zeit mit seiner Liebsten zu
verbringen und einen guten Kaffee am Morgen.
Es war ihm überhaupt nicht bewusst, dass viele
ihn wohl um seine Normalität beneideten.

———

Si vedeva come un tipo normale con desideri
molto comuni. Gli piaceva trascorrere il tempo
con la sua amata e un buon caffè al mattino.
Non si rendeva conto che molti dovevano
invidiare la sua normalità.

———

№ 64
Gaston

———

He was never a star at algebra, but realized
over and over again that life comes with pluses
and minuses, a constant flux of highs and lows.
The most critical lesson he learned from this
truth is that miracles come out of struggles.

———

Er war nie eine Leuchte in Algebra, stellte aber
immer wieder erneut fest, dass das Leben viele
Plus- und viele Minusmomente bietet, ein steter
Fluss aus Höhen und Tiefen. Die wichtigste
Erkenntnis, die er aus dieser Wahrheit zog,
ist, dass Wunder aus Anstrengungen heraus
entstehen.

———

Non era mai stato un asso in algebra, eppure
constatò ripetute volte che la vita è fatta di più
e meno, un costante flusso di alti e bassi.
La lezione più dura che ha imparato da questa
verità è che i miracoli nascono dalle battaglie.

———

nº 65
Boris

———

Looking back, being color-blind had been
hard for someone like him, All those green
flags he had ignored must have been red
ones warning him.

———

Rückblickend war es schwierig gewesen
für jemanden wie ihn, farbenblind zu sein.
All diese grünen Fahnen, die er ignoriert
hatte, mussten wohl rote gewesen sein,
die ihn warnten.

———

Ripensandoci, non riconoscere i colori era
stato difficile per uno come lui. Tutte quelle
bandiere verdi che aveva ignorato
devono essere state segnali rossi che
lo mettevano in guardia.

———

———

He was a smart one. He could read personalities
the moment they walked into the room.
He adjusted his performance according to his
own agenda. If they took a good look at him,
they would never see a real smile or
genuine emotion.

———

Er war geschickt. Er durchschaute
Persönlichkeiten, sobald sie den Raum betraten.
Sein Auftreten passte er seiner eigenen Agenda
an. Wenn sie ihn genau betrachteten, würden
sie niemals ein echtes Lächeln oder ein
aufrichtiges Gefühl sehen.

———

Era uno intelligente. Sapeva leggere la
personalità delle persone nel momento in cui
entravano nella sua stanza. Regolava la sua
prestazione secondo la sua agenda personale.
Se lo avessero guardato bene, non avrebbero
mai trovato un sorriso vero o un'emozione
genuina.

———

nº 67
Massimo

———

Feeling like a victim was tearing him apart.
He couldn't understand why someone had hurt
him so badly. What if he became the villain
instead? He tried and understood how good
harming felt. But he stopped before he got
addicted to it. This was not who he was, and he
wanted to leave some work for karma.

———

Sich wie ein Opfer zu fühlen, zerriss ihn
innerlich. Er konnte nicht begreifen, warum
ihn jemand so sehr verletzt hatte. Was, wenn
er stattdessen der Bösewicht wurde? Er
versuchte es und verstand, wie gut es sich
anfühlte, zu verletzen. Aber er ließ es wieder
sein, bevor er süchtig danach wurde. Dies war
nicht seine Art und er wollte für das Karma
noch etwas Arbeit übrig lassen.

———

Sentirsi una vittima lo stava facendo a pezzi.
Non riusciva a capire perché qualcuno lo avesse
ferito a quel modo. E se diventasse lui il cattivo?
Ci provò e capì quale bella sensazione desse il
fare male. Ma la smise prima che diventasse un
vizio. Lui non era fatto così, inoltre desiderava
lasciare un po' di lavoro per il karma.

———

n° 68
Luis

———

He was a very good listener. This gave others
the feeling that they were valued and special.
They came from far and wide for his
wise advice.

———

Er war ein sehr guter Zuhörer. Das gab anderen
das Gefühl, geschätzt und außergewöhnlich
zu sein. Von nah und fern kamen sie zu ihm,
um seinen klugen Rat einzuholen.

———

Era un bravissimo ascoltatore. Ciò dava agli
altri la sensazione di essere apprezzati e
speciali. Venivano da ogni dove per i suoi
saggi consigli.

———

nº 69
Hussein

———

Safety was most important for him. He had
never felt safe in his younger years. While his
faith in others was being tested over and over,
he could have given up. Little by little he learned
what to search for and finally feel safe.

———

Sicherheit war für ihn das Wichtigste.
Er hatte sich in seinen jungen Jahren nie
wirklich geborgen gefühlt. Während sein
Vertrauen in andere immer wieder aufs Neue
auf die Probe gestellt wurde, wollte er jeder
Mal fast aufgeben. Nach und nach lernte er,
wonach er suchen musste, um sich endlich
geborgen und sicher zu fühlen.

———

La sicurezza era molto importante per lui.
Non si era mai sentito sicuro da giovane.
Mentre la sua fiducia negli altri continuava
a essere messa alla prova, avrebbe potuto
arrendersi. Poco a poco imparò cosa cercare
per sentirsi alla fine sicuro.

———

№ 70
Raife

———

He really thought his best was enough.
But the title of "the best" was already taken
by Mr. Knowitall. He needed to come up with
another purpose in life. "Good" seemed to fit
the bill. He heard his mother say we need
more of that in this world.

———

Er dachte wirklich, sein Bestes wäre gut genug.
Aber den Titel „Der Beste" hatte bereits Herr
Besserwisser für sich vereinnahmt. Er musste
sich eine andere Aufgabe im Leben suchen.
„Gut zu sein" schien hervorragend zu passen.
Er hörte seine Mutter sagen: „Wir brauchen
mehr davon in dieser Welt."

———

Pensava davvero che il suo essere "meglio"
fosse sufficiente. Ma il titolo di "migliore" era
già stato preso dal signor Sotutto. Aveva bisogno
di trovare un altro scopo nella vita. Il "bene"
sembrava essere quello giusto. Sentiva sua
madre dire che dovrebbe essercene di più
a questo mondo.

———

№ 71
Margaret

———

Cooking is her greatest talent. Big contrasts in
taste like sweet and salty is the secret formula
to all her recipes. Her favorite saying is, "Adding
Bacon always creates magic!"

———

Beim Kochen zeigt sie ihr größtes Talent.
Geschmackliche Kontraste wie süß und salzig
sind die Zauberformel all ihrer Gerichte.
Ihr Motto lautet: „Speck sorgt immer für
den magischen Kick!"

———

Cucinare è il suo più grande talento.
I forti contrasti di sapore come dolce e salato
sono la formula segreta di tutte le sue ricette.
Il suo modo di dire preferito: "Aggiungere
della pancetta dà sempre un tocco di magia".

———

№ 72
Liz

————

She had had her heart broken so many times
that she decided to fall in love with sunsets
instead. Every day she had a new love and also
a new good-bye. When the good-byes became
bearable, someone fell in love with her.

————

Ihr Herz war schon so oft gebrochen worden,
dass sie beschloss, sich stattdessen in
Sonnenuntergänge zu verlieben. Jeden Tag
fand sie eine neue Liebe und nahm erneut
Abschied. Als das Abschiednehmen erträglich
wurde, verliebte sich jemand in sie.

————

Le si era spezzato il cuore così tante volte che
decise di innamorarsi piuttosto dei tramonti.
Ogni giorno viveva un amore nuovo e un nuovo
addio. Quando gli addii divennero sopportabili,
qualcuno si innamorò di lei.

————

№ 73
Lewis

———

He enjoys the sensation of rain falling on the
leaves in his garden. It takes him back to his
childhood. Must grandpa have realized that
with kindness and education someone
will always be remembered?

———

Er genießt das Gefühl, wenn in seinem Garten
der Regen auf die Blätter fällt. Es bringt ihn
zurück in seine Kindheit. Ob Großvater wusste,
dass man sich mit Freundlichkeit und Erziehung
unauslöschlich einprägt?

———

Ama la sensazione della pioggia che cade
sulle foglie nel suo giardino. Lo riporta alla
sua infanzia. Il nonno aveva capito che con la
gentilezza e la buona educazione una persona
viene ricordata per sempre?

———

№ 74
Ludivine

———

She had longed to become a mother, a better
one than she had had herself. She found a
good-hearted but boring husband and had
two kids. However, when she was tired of
playing the housewife, she divorced him and
demanded child support. Wasn't she the winner
of them all?

———

Sie hatte sich danach gesehnt, Mutter zu
werden, und zwar eine bessere als ihre eigene
es war. Sie fand einen gutmütigen, aber
langweiligen Mann und bekam zwei Kinder.
Als sie es jedoch leid war, die Hausfrau zu
spielen, ließ sie sich von ihm scheiden und
forderte Unterhalt für die Kinder. War sie
nicht die Gewinnerin von allen?

———

Aveva tanto desiderato diventare madre,
una migliore di quella che aveva avuto lei.
Si trovò un marito di buon cuore ma noioso,
ed ebbe due figli. Tuttavia, quando si stufò
di giocare alla casalinga, divorziò da lui e
pretese il mantenimento dei figli. Non è
stata lei la vincitrice fra tutti?

———

nº 75
Morton

———

He wasn't afraid of blood or pain. He always
said we are all going to die one day when
questioned about the ethics of bullfighting.
How could he ever have imagined reincarnation
was best friends with karma and eternity,
when they talked about planning his
spirit's future.

———

Er fürchtete weder Blut noch Schmerzen.
Auf die Frage nach der Ethik des Stierkampfes
sagte er immer, wir alle würden eines Tages
sterben. Wie hatte er sich jemals vorstellen
können, dass Reinkarnation auf du und du mit
Karma und Ewigkeit stand, wenn es darum ging,
die Zukunft seines Geistes zu planen.

———

Non aveva paura del sangue o del dolore.
Se interrogato sull'etica della tauromachia,
diceva sempre che tutti, un giorno, dobbiamo
morire. Come avrebbe mai potuto immaginare
che la reincarnazione fosse la migliore amica
del karma e dell'eternità, quando si parlava
di pianificare il futuro del suo spirito.

———

№ 76
Fae

———

Being a single mother, she had been the talk
of the village for years. She tried to raise the little
one all by herself. But when destiny took him
away from her, none of the villagers had enough
courage or kindness to comfort a grieving
mother. Confronting this reality prompted her
to start over somewhere else.

———

Als alleinerziehende Mutter war sie im
Dorf jahrelang das Gesprächsthema gewesen.
Sie hatte versucht, den Kleinen ganz allein
großzuziehen. Als aber das Schicksal ihn ihr
nahm, hatte keiner der Dorfbewohner genug
Courage oder Barmherzigkeit, eine trauernde
Mutter zu trösten. Als sie dies erkannte, fasste sie
den Entschluss, woanders neu anzufangen.

———

Essendo una madre single, per anni era stata
oggetto di conversazione nel villaggio. Cercò
di crescere il piccolo da sola. Ma quando il
destino glielo portò via, nessuno degli abitanti
del paese ebbe il coraggio o la gentilezza di
consolare una madre in lutto. Confrontandosi
con questa realtà, decise prontamente
di ricominciare altrove.

———

nº 77
Buster

———

He loves magic. The trick of mysteriously
disappearing is his all time favorite. Everytime
he vanishes, he wonders if they will ever
remember him.

———

Er liebt die Zauberei. Auf unerklärliche Weise zu
verschwinden ist sein absoluter Lieblingstrick.
Jedes Mal, wenn er verschwindet, fragt er sich,
ob man sich jemals an ihn erinnern wird.

———

Ama la magia. Il trucco della scomparsa
misteriosa è il suo preferito. Ogni volta che
scompare, si chiede se si ricorderanno
mai di lui.

———

nº 78
João

———

He knew all about his rights. And liked to
point the finger when someone didn't fulfill
his duty. He never ever thought about his own
responsibilities. Couldn't they see from
a distance how great he was?

———

Er wusste alles über seine Rechte. Und er zeigte
gern mit dem Finger darauf, wenn jemand
seiner Pflicht nicht nachkam. Über seine eigene
Verantwortung dachte er niemals nach.
Sah man denn nicht schon aus der Ferne,
wie großartig er war?

———

Sapeva tutto riguardo i suoi diritti. E gli piaceva
puntare il dito quando qualcuno non rispettava
il proprio dovere. Non aveva mai pensato alle
sue responsabilità. Non si vedeva sin da
lontano quanto fosse grande?

———

№ 79
stu

———

He knew about diversity. Some were black;
others were white. He was happy to be
somewhere in between. Avoiding the ones
that weren't kind had always been his
favorite game.

———

Er wusste von der Vielfalt. Einige waren
schwarz, andere weiß. Er war froh, irgendwo
dazwischen zu liegen. Denjenigen aus dem
Weg zu gehen, die nicht nett waren, war
immer schon sein Lieblingsspiel.

———

Conosceva la diversità. Alcuni erano neri,
altri bianchi. Era contento di trovarsi in qualche
punto a metà strada. Evitare le persone che non
erano gentili era sempre stato il suo
gioco preferito.

———

№ 80
steph

———

Unfortunately she had never been the prettiest
girl in town. Stephanie pushes and drags her
pretty daughter into situations where she wishes
she had been herself. It is only a matter of time
before this story is interrupted by the willpower
of a strong young girl with a mind of her own.

———

Zu ihrem Leidwesen war sie nie das hübscheste
Mädchen der Stadt gewesen. Jetzt drängt
Stephanie ihre hübsche Tochter in jene
Situationen, die sie selbst so gern erlebt hätte.
Es ist nur eine Frage der Zeit, bis die Willenskraft
eines jungen Mädchens mit einem eigenen Kopf
diesem Spiel ein Ende bereitet.

———

Purtroppo non era mai stata la ragazza più bella
della città. Stephanie spinge e trascina la sua
bella figlia in situazioni in cui vorrebbe essersi
trovata lei. È solo questione di tempo prima
che questa storia abbia fine per volontà di una
giovane ragazza forte e con le proprie idee.

———

nº 81
zero

———

Unfortunately she was born on the wrong
side of the planet. She has to work long hours
creating cheap goods that others more fortunate
buy and replace if they get bored. Her reason to
be is a question she never asks herself.

———

Leider wurde sie auf der falschen Seite des
Planeten geboren. Sie musste viele Stunden
arbeiten, um billige Waren herzustellen, die
andere, die mehr Glück hatten, kaufen und
wieder ersetzen, wenn es ihnen langweilig wird.
Die Frage nach dem Sinn ihres Lebens ist eine
Frage, die sie sich niemals stellt.

———

Purtroppo è nata nella parte sbagliata del
pianeta. Deve lavorare a lungo per realizzare
prodotti a buon mercato che altri più fortunati
di lei acquistano e sostituiscono quando ne sono
stufi. La sua ragione d'essere è una domanda
che non si pone mai.

———

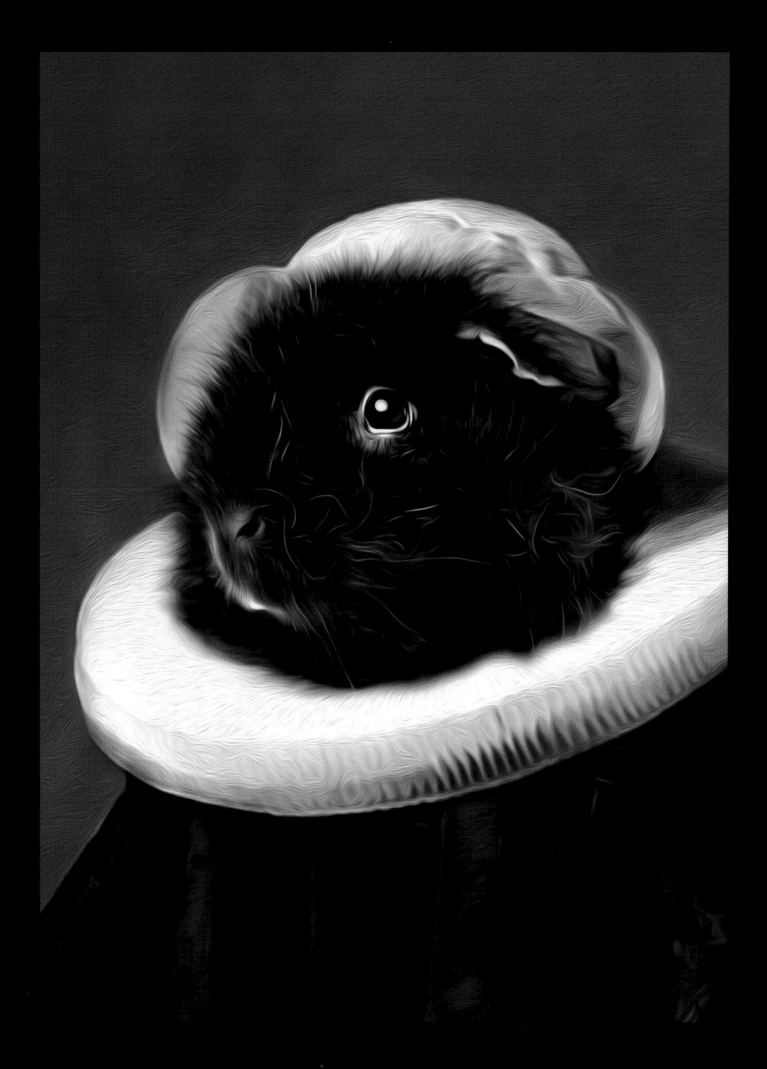

№ 82
Paolo

———

His hobby is planting seeds in the minds of those who are sad and lost to give them dreams for their future. It is a secret pleasure for him to see those magical dreams come true.

———

Sein Hobby ist es, jenen, die traurig und verloren sind, Samen in den Kopf zu setzen, aus denen in ihnen Träume für die Zukunft keimen. Es ist eine geheime Freude zu sehen, wie diese magischen Träume wahr werden.

———

Il suo hobby è piantare semi nella mente di coloro che sono tristi e smarriti per donare loro sogni per il futuro. È un piacere segreto per lui vedere quei sogni magici diventare realtà.

———

№ 83
Margit

———

She had always hated complainers. But when
tragedy hit her, the pain wouldn't go away.
Her friends expected her to smile and act like
sunshine. They didn't realize how much time she
needed. After recovering she valued different
qualities in her friendships.

———

Sie hatte die Leute, die immer nur jammern,
stets verabscheut. Als sie jedoch selbst von
einer Tragödie betroffen war, ging der Schmerz
einfach nicht weg. Ihre Freunde erwarteten
von ihr, dass sie lächelte und strahlte. Sie
merkten nicht, wie viel Zeit sie brauchte. Als es
ihr wieder besser ging, schätzte sie bei ihren
Freundschaften andere Eigenschaften.

———

Aveva sempre odiato le persone che si
lamentano. Ma quando la tragedia la colpì,
il dolore non voleva andarsene. I suoi amici si
aspettavano che sorridesse e fosse raggiante.
Non si rendevano conto di quanto tempo le
servisse. Dopo essersi ripresa, apprezzò
qualità diverse nelle proprie amicizie.

———

————

Every day after cleaning the whole house,
she wished her mum was there to be proud
of the result. She just doesn't realize that in fact
all she longed for was for her mother to tell
her she loved her.

————

Jeden Tag nach dem Hausputz wünschte sie
sich, ihre Mutter wäre da, um stolz auf das
Ergebnis zu sein. Sie merkt dabei gar nicht, dass
sie sich eigentlich nur nach ihrer Mutter sehnt,
die ihr sagt, dass sie sie liebt.

————

Ogni giorno, dopo aver pulito tutta la casa,
desiderava che la madre fosse lì per essere
orgogliosa del risultato. Non riesce a capire
che in realtà non desiderava altro che la
madre le dicesse che le voleva bene.

————

№ 85
Rudolph

———

He was always after something new: another
new girlfriend, another new job. Only after
losing it all, he realized what he needed all along.
Just loving himself was enough.

———

Er war immer auf etwas Neues aus: noch eine
neue Freundin, noch einen neuen Job. Erst
nachdem er alles verloren hatte, wurde ihm
bewusst, was er eigentlich brauchte. Einfach
sich selbst zu lieben, war genug.

———

Cercava sempre qualcosa di nuovo: una nuova
ragazza, un nuovo lavoro. Solo dopo aver
perso tutto, capì di che cosa avesse bisogno fin
dall'inizio. Bastava amare sé stesso.

———

№ 86
Esteban

———

Being creative has always been his passion.
Becoming an artist was an easy choice. Today's
customers prefer decoration. They know what
they want and don't realize it is not art without
the artist's mind. Will he be creative enough to
make them see his point of view?

———

Kreativ zu sein, war immer schon seine
Leidenschaft. Künstler zu werden, war eine
einfache Entscheidung. Heutzutage geht es
Kunden mehr um Dekoration. Sie wissen, was
sie wollen und merken nicht, dass es keine
Kunst gibt ohne den Geist des Künstlers. Wird
er kreativ genug sein, sie seine Sicht der Dinge
erkennen zu lassen.

———

Essere creativo è sempre stata la sua passione.
Diventare un artista è stata una scelta facile.
Oggi i clienti preferiscono le decorazioni. Sanno
quello che vogliono e non capiscono che non c'è
arte senza la mente dell'artista. Sarà abbastanza
creativo da far loro capire il suo punto di vista?

———

№ 87
Björn

He was getting way too big for her to carry him around. He was a sweet kid with no other curiosity about the world. Life with mum felt good and safe. Mum bought him a puppy, just so he could learn about taking care of something. He remembers this as the best thing that ever happened to him.

Er war viel zu groß, um noch von ihr herumgetragen zu werden. Er war ein sanftes Kind ohne große Ansprüche an die Welt. Das Leben mit Mama war gut und sicher. Sie kaufte ihm eine Puppe, sodass er lernen konnte, sich um irgendetwas zu kümmern. Er erinnert sich daran als das Beste, was ihm je widerfahren war.

Stava diventando troppo grande perché lei lo portasse in giro. Era un bambino dolce, senza altra curiosità nei confronti del mondo. Con la mamma si sentiva bene e al sicuro. La mamma gli comprò un cucciolo, in modo che imparasse a prendersi cura di qualcosa. Lui se ne ricorda come la cosa migliore che gli sia mai capitata.

№ 88
stag

The doctor said it was depression and he
had to keep a diary. While staring at the ceiling,
he discovered a complete upside-down world
that triggered his imagination. After his first
novel was published, he thanked his doctor.
He figured it had not been a depression that
had hit him so hard, but reality.

Der Arzt hatte gesagt, es wäre eine Depression
und er solle Tagebuch führen. Während er an die
Decke starrte, entdeckte er eine völlig verdrehte
Welt, die seine Fantasie beflügelte. Nachdem sein
erster Roman erschienen war, bedankte er sich
bei seinem Arzt. Er schätzte, es war weniger eine
Depression, die ihn so sehr mitgenommen hatte,
als vielmehr die Realität.

Il medico disse che si trattava di depressione e
che doveva tenere un diario. Fissando il soffitto,
scoprì un mondo completamente sottosopra
che scatenò la sua immaginazione. Dopo la
pubblicazione del suo primo romanzo, ringraziò
il suo medico. Lui comprese che non era stata la
depressione ad abbatterlo così, ma la realtà.

+ 1
salvador

———

Magical things started to happen on his journey.
Feeling sad was no longer necessary once he
had decided to follow his heart. Just to love and
be loved in return was all he needed to discover.

———

Auf seiner Reise ergaben sich wundersame
Dinge. Traurig zu sein, war unnötig geworden,
nachdem er beschlossen hatte, seinem Herzen
zu folgen. Alles, was er entdecken musste, war
zu lieben und geliebt zu werden.

———

Durante il suo viaggio cominciarono ad
accadere cose magiche. Non dovette più sentirsi
triste una volta deciso di seguire il proprio cuore.
Amare ed essere contraccambiati era tutto ciò
che aveva bisogno di scoprire.

———

acknowledgments

———

A curious thank you to the person who unlocked the extra talent I had no idea I owned, who carefully twisted my truth for over seven years, who didn't let me finish my sentences and made me question myself. We lived according to a list of made-up rules i had never received before we started and which changed constantly. I was stupid and naive and was not aware of your bigger plan. I pity you that you aren't able to feel. It must be very miserable and lonely inside.

This thank you is not meant to sound like self pity. I thought about not mentioning it at all, but I find it is important to speak up for all those people who are or have been in similar situations. I am happy to have realised that forward is the only way to go. Every day I am convinced this is the right direction.

You also gifted me with more curiosity about others and made me wiser. I try more and more to keep my sensitivity and not to be judgemental. I would never want to become like you. Nobody is perfect and perfection is very boring anyhow. Every cloud has a silver lining.

TEIN LUCASSON

danke

———

Ein ungewöhnlicher Dank geht an die Person, die das gewisse Talent, von dem ich keine Ahnung hatte, es zu besitzen, herauslockte, die mehr als sieben Jahre lang sorgfältig meine Wahrheit verdrehte, mich meine Sätze nicht vollenden ließ und dafür sorgte, dass ich mich selbst in Frage stellte. Wir lebten nach einer Liste aufgestellter Regeln, die ich zuvor nie erhalten hatte und die sich ständig veränderte. Ich war dumm und naiv und mir deines größeren Plans nicht bewusst. Ich habe Mitleid mit dir, dass du nicht fühlen kannst. Es muss sich im Inneren sehr unglücklich und einsam anfühlen.

Dieser Dank soll nicht nach Selbstmitleid klingen. Ich hatte überlegt, es gar nicht zu erwähnen, finde aber, es ist wichtig, für all jene einzutreten, die in ähnlichen Situationen waren oder sind. Ich bin froh, mir bewusst geworden zu sein, dass der Weg nach vorne der einzig mögliche ist. Tagtäglich bin ich überzeugt davon, dass dies die richtige Richtung ist.

Du hast in mir auch mehr Neugier auf andere geweckt und mich weiser gemacht. Ich bemühe mich zunehmend darum, mir meine Sensibilität zu bewahren und nicht voreingenommen zu sein. Ich würde niemals so werden wollen wie du. Niemand ist perfekt und Perfektion ist sowieso sehr langweilig. Hinter jeder Wolke ist ein Silberstreif.

TEIN LUCASSON

ringraziamenti

—

Un ringraziamento singolare va alla persona che ha fatto emergere un talento nascosto che non avevo idea di possedere, che ha accuratamente distorto la mia realtà per più di sette anni e che non mi lasciava finire di parlare, facendomi mettere in dubbio me stesso. Abbiamo vissuto secondo una serie di regole prestabilite che non avevo mai ricevuto prima che cominciassimo e che cambiavano in continuazione. Ero stupido e ingenuo, ed inconsapevole del tuo piano più ampio. Ti compatisco per la tua mancanza di sensibilità. Dentro deve esserci tanta tristezza e solitudine.

Questo ringraziamento non vuole essere un'autocommiserazione. Avevo pensato di non menzionarlo affatto, ma credo che sia importante parlare per tutte le persone che si trovano o si sono trovate in situazioni simili. Sono contento di aver capito che guardare avanti è l'unica via da prendere. Ogni giorno sono convinto che sia questa la direzione giusta.

A te devo anche il mio senso di curiosità nei confronti degli altri e la mia maggior saggezza. Mi sforzo in continuazione di mantenere la mia sensibilità e di non giudicare. Non vorrei mai diventare come te. Nessuno è perfetto, e in ogni caso la perfezione è noiosa. Anche le cose peggiori hanno un risvolto positivo.

TEIN LUCASSON

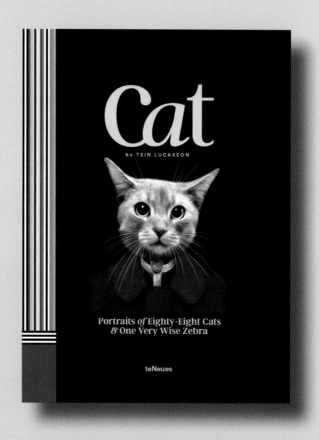

soon
to come
——

BIRD
——

89 stories
about:
*wise
helpers*

——

EXPECTED
2021

imprint

——

Text and Pictures by Tein Lucasson
(with a special thanks to Roisin Tambour)
Copyediting (English) by Maria Regina Madarang
Translations (German) by Claudia Theis-Passaro
Translations (Italian) by Federica Benetti (WeSwitch
Languages)
Design by Tein Lucasson
Editorial coordination by Roman Korn
Production by Sandra Jansen-Dorn
Color separation by Jens Grundei

ISBN 978-3-96171-290-8

Library of Congress Number: 2020936048

Printed in the Czech Republic by Tesinska Tiskarna AG

Bibliographic information published by the Deutsche
Nationalbibliothek
The Deutsche Nationalbibliothek lists this publication in
the Deutsche Nationalbibliografie; detailed bibliographic
data are available on the Internet at http://dnb.dnb.de.

Published by teNeues Publishing Group

teNeues Media GmbH & Co. KG
Am Selder 37, 47906 Kempen, Germany
Phone: +49-(0)2152-916-0
Fax: +49-(0)2152-916-111
E-mail: books@teneues.com

Press department: Andrea Rehn
Phone: +49-(0)2152-916-202
E-mail: arehn@teneues.com

teNeues Media GmbH & Co. KG
Munich Office
Pilotystrasse 4, 80538 Munich, Germany
Phone: +49-(0)89-443-8889-62
E-mail: bkellner@teneues.com

Berlin Office
Mommsenstrasse 43, 10629 Berlin, Germany
Phone: +49 (0)1520 8 51 10 64
E-mail: ajasper@teneues.com

teNeues Publishing Company
350 7th Avenue, Suite 301, New York, NY 10001, USA
Phone: +1-212-627-9090
Fax: +1-212-627-9511

teNeues Publishing UK Ltd.
12 Ferndene Road, London SE24 0AQ, UK
Phone: +44-(0)20-3542-8997

teNeues France S.A.R.L.
39, rue des Billets, 18250 Henrichemont, France
Phone: +33-(0)2-4826-9348
Fax: +33-(0)1-7072-3482

www.teneues.com

teNeues Publishing Group
Kempen
Berlin
London
Munich
New York
Paris

teNeues